Motorcycles
A first-time buyer's guide

Also from Veloce Publishing

RAC handbooks

Caring for your car – How to maintain & service your car (Fry)
Caring for your car's bodywork and interior (Nixon)
Caring for your bicycle – How to maintain & repair your bicycle (Henshaw)
Dogs on wheels – Travelling with your canine companion (Mort)
How your motorcycle works – Your guide to the components & systems of modern
    motorcycles (Henshaw)
Caring for your scooter – How to maintain & service your 49cc to 125cc twist & go
    scooter (Fry)
Efficient Driver's Handbook, The (Moss)
Electric Cars – The Future is Now! (Linde)
First aid for your car – Your expert guide to common problems & how to fix them
    (Collins)
How your car works (Linde)
Motorcycles – A first-time-buyer's guide (Henshaw)
Motorhomes – A first-time-buyer's guide (Fry)
Pass the MoT test! – How to check & prepare your car for the annual MoT test
    (Paxton)
Selling your car – How to make your car look great and how to sell it fast (Knight)
Simple fixes for your car – How to do small jobs for yourself and save money
    (Collins)

This publication has been produced on behalf of RAC by Veloce Publishing LTD. The views and the opinions expressed by the author are entirely his own, and do not necessarily reflect those of RAC. New automotive technology is constantly emerging; the information in this book reflects the status quo at the date of publication.

www.rac.co.uk
www.veloce.co.uk

First published in December 2012 by Veloce Publishing Limited, Veloce House, Parkway Farm Business Park, Middle Farm Way, Poundbury, Dorchester, Dorset, DT1 3AR, England.
Fax 01305 250479/e-mail info@veloce.co.uk/web www.veloce.co.uk or www.velocebooks.com.

ISBN: 978-1-845844-95-0 UPC: 6-36847-04495-4

Readers with ideas for automotive books, or books on other transport or related hobby subjects, are invited to write to the editorial director of Veloce Publishing at the above address.
British Library Cataloguing in Publication Data – A catalogue record for this book is available from the British Library.
Typesetting, design and page make-up all by Veloce Publishing Ltd on Apple Mac. Printed in India by Imprint Digital.

Motorcycles
A first-time buyer's guide

Peter Henshaw

Contents

Introduction

Acknowledgements

Thanks go to all those people and organisations whose pictures are used in this book. So, in no particular order: Triumph Motorcycles, Harley-Davidson, Black Horse Finance, Suzuki GB, Driving Standards Agency, Motorcycle Industry Association, Fabulous Biker Boys, Yamaha UK, Honda UK, National Association of Bikers with a Disability, the IAM, and Rona Bell. Thanks also to Anna Finch for additional photography.

Why ride?

This book is intended for those people who are thinking of buying their first motorcycle or scooter, but who have never ridden one before. Whether you're looking for a means of commuting to work or college, to the shops, for some fun at the weekends, or longer distance riding, this book is a complete guide, from applying for your licence through buying a bike to taking advanced training.

Buying your first motorcycle, riding it, taking care of it, and meeting other bikers will add another facet to your life. Like no other form of transport (though cycling runs a close second) it can turn the mundane business of travelling from A to B into a mini adventure, an intense experience that will never leave you bored, or longing for the journey to end.

Of course, riding a bike has its downsides too – it can be wet, cold, and high-risk – though all of these things can be minimised with the right kit, training and attitude. There's no doubt that riding a motorcycle is a higher risk activity than driving a car or sitting on a train. Alongside cyclists, motorcyclists are the most vulnerable road users of all, without a cage of metal to protect them, not to mention seatbelts and airbags.

Learning to ride is well worth the effort.
(Courtesy MCIA)

However, this risk can be minimised through training. Today, every new rider has to undertake proper training before heading out onto the road. After passing the test, there are plenty of opportunities to take further training for advanced riding. And the best motorcycle kit – clothing, helmet and gloves – will do a lot to protect you in the event of a crash. Most of it is also very waterproof – there's no guarantee that you will never get wet and/or cold, but modern kit will go a long way to preventing both.

Having got the downsides out of the way, we can address the many advantages of biking. It's often seen as an impractical form of transport – the need to wear special

It's official – motorcycling is fun!

clothing, the lack of luggage space – but in towns and cities, two-wheelers have plenty of practical advantages. You won't get stuck in traffic – the joy of gliding steadily past stationary queues of cars is something to savour on the way to work. There's no faster means of transport through heavy traffic, and you won't have to break any speed limits. Parking, so long as you stick to designated bike bays, is usually free, and bikes can often be tucked away into odd corners that cars can't. If you live in London, don't forget that all motorcycles and scooters are exempt from the Congestion Charge. The green credentials of bikes are sometimes overstated, but there's no doubt that a small/mid-sized bike is a greener option than a car. It will use less fuel, emit less CO2, take up less road space, and contribute less to congestion.

Mile-for-mile, most motorcycles are cheaper to run than most cars. Tyres and brake pads don't last so long, but small bikes, in particular, don't use much fuel (100mpg or more is typical for a 125), insurance for many low cc bikes is cheaper than for a car, and, as I said earlier, you'll rarely get charged for

parking. Note, though, that insurance on bikes over 600cc can be just as expensive as a car for younger riders.

That's the practical stuff, but it's the emotional side of biking that brings the biggest rewards. First off, there's the sheer intensity of riding a bike. In a car, you're sitting in a box, detached from the machinery. On a bike, you are part of it, using your whole body weight to steer it and make the tiniest adjustments, interacting with it every second. Then there's the fresh air feeling. Even fully kitted-up and with a full-face helmet, you still feel out in the elements, and part of them – smell the fresh mown grass, hear the birds singing – it may sound like a cliché, but it's true. And there's still a strong feeling of camaraderie among motorcyclists – it's not compulsory to wave at every biker that passes, but if feels good when you do.

Finally, maybe it's all best summed up by a poster campaign run by the Motorcycle Industry Association back in the 1990s. It showed a rider on a bright yellow bike, riding through sunshine past a field of corn. The strapline read: 'Free with every motorcycle – You.'

one
Rules & regulations

How to get a licence

The route to getting a bike licence and getting on the road seems complicated, but it really isn't. Which route you take depends on your age and the type of bike you want to ride. At age 16, you can ride a moped, which has an engine of less than 50cc and a maximum top speed of 31mph (28mph on 2003-on EU-approved mopeds). You will need a provisional licence (apply at the Post Office or online at www.dvla.gov.uk) and you will have to pass CBT (see page 12) before riding on the road with L-plates. If you want to ditch the L-plates or carry a passenger, you'll need to pass the Theory and Practical tests first.

Reverse of the photocard licence shows which class of vehicle you can drive: M = Moped, A1 = Motorcycle, up to 125cc/14.6bhp, A2 = Motorcycle, up to 33bhp (46.6bhp from January 2013), A = Motorcycle licence, unlimited.

Photocard licence must be updated with a new photo every ten years.

At 17 or over, you have two routes to getting a full licence – if 21 or over, there's a third route as well – Direct Access. In all cases, you will need to pass CBT, the Theory test and Practical test.

1) A1 licence. If you only want to ride a small motorcycle up to 125cc, you can train and take CBT, then the Theory/Practical tests on a 75-125cc bike. If you pass, you can ride a bike up to 125cc and 14.6bhp – almost every 125cc bike comes into this 'learner legal' category. You can also carry a passenger and ride on motorways.

2) A2 licence. If you're planning to ride a bigger bike, take this route. Train and take the Theory/Practical tests on a bike of 120-125cc, capable of reaching at least 62mph. Pass the tests, and you can ride any motorcycle up to 33bhp. You can carry a passenger, ride on motorways, and don't need L-plates. After two years, your A2 licence becomes a full A licence, whereupon you can ride any motorcycle, with no power limit. If you hit 21 within that two years, and can't wait, you can take the Practical test again on a bike of at least 46.6bhp – then you can ride whatever you like.

From 19 January 2013, the law changes. The A2 licence now covers bikes up to 46.6bhp, but you must be aged 19 or over, and take the Practical test on a bike of 33-46.6bhp and 395cc or over.

3) A licence. If you are 21 or over, you can 'fast track' straight to a bigger bike by taking Direct Access. Training and testing are on a combination of 125cc and bigger bikes. If you want, you can train on your own on an up to 125cc bike, with L-plates, but to train on anything bigger on the road, you must be accompanied by a qualified instructor. The test must be done on a bike of at least 46.6bhp – your trainer will usually provide this bike as part of the package. After passing the Practical test, you have a full A licence, and can ride whatever you like.

From 19 January 2013, the law changes. You need to be aged 24 or over to do Direct Access. If you are 21 or over and have two years' experience on an A2 licence, you can gain an A licence by taking the Practical test again. In both cases, you must take the test on a bike of at least 53.6bhp and over 595cc. Further changes in power limits are due for A, A1 and A2 licences at the end of 2013 – check for the current licence requirements at www.dft.gov.uk/dsa.

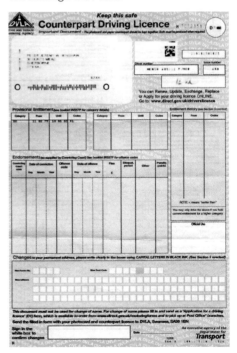

Counterpart (paper) licence should be kept in a safe place.

Note that if you pass your Practical test on a twist-and-go (automatic transmission) scooter, you will have a licence for automatics only, and will not be qualified to ride a bike with clutch and manual gears – to do that, you'll have to take the Practical test on a bike with manual gear change, although there's no problem riding a manual scooter.

Finally, the licence requirements for riding a motorcycle and sidecar are exactly the same as those for a solo bike.

Can I ride on a full car licence?

No. Your full car licence will have a provisional motorcycle entitlement, but to make use of it you will have to pass CBT at least (see page 12), and if you want a full motorcycle licence you will have to take one of the three routes detailed previously. But there are two exceptions:

The Piaggio MP3 LT three-wheeled scooter can be ridden on a car licence.

Exception 1 – Mopeds: If you obtained your full car licence before 1st February 2001, you can head straight out onto the road on a speed restricted moped – you can carry a passenger and don't need L-plates.

Exception 2 – Piaggio MP3 LT: The Piaggio MP3 is a three-wheeled scooter (two front wheels, one rear) that tilts to corner, just like a two-wheeler. It's a great idea with superb roadholding, though not cheap. The special LT version is classed as a motor tricycle, and, as such, can be ridden by any holder of a full car licence – there's no need to take any training, pass CBT or a test. A word of warning – if buying one of these secondhand, make sure it really is the LT version, as the standard MP3 is classed as a scooter, and you'll need to take the usual two-wheel licence routes to ride it. The LT has a brake pedal as well as the usual handlebar levers. Also, if you really haven't had any two-wheel experience, it's highly recommended that you take some training before heading out onto the road on your MP3 LT. At the time of writing, this scooter is the only one in the tricycle category.

Note that three-wheeled motorcycles (often referred to as 'trikes') do not come into this category. These are the ones, often home-built, usually with one wheel in front, two behind, which do not lean in corners. From 19 January 2013, these are in the same licence category as motorcycles, and the licence requirements are the same.

Finding a trainer

There are about 600 trainers across the UK who offer pre-test motorcycle training. They have to be approved by

CBT covers basic motorcycle control, on-road and on-site. (DSA Crown Copyright)

the Driving Standards Agency, which guarantees minimum standards. Some are also members of the Motorcycle Industry Trainers Association. Find your nearest trainer through the official Government website (www.direct.gov. uk), through the MCITA site (www.mcita. co.uk), or the Yellow Pages.

What is CBT?

CBT – Compulsory Basic Training – is a pre-test that you have to pass before taking the Theory/Practical tests. It's the first step towards getting a full motorcycle licence.

CBT is provided by training schools, which must be approved by the Driving Standards Agency (DSA). The whole thing takes most of a day, and you must wear riding kit – helmet, gloves and jacket as a minimum. There are five main sections, starting with a classroom session before being given some basic

on-site riding training. Then it's back to the classroom for more theory before finally heading out onto the road with your instructor. You'll be started off on quieter roads before moving onto busier ones.

Once your instructor is convinced you're safe to ride on your own, you'll be issued with a CBT Certificate (DL196, to give its official title). This enables you to ride a bike up to 125cc on the road, with L-plates, unaccompanied. It's valid for two years. If you haven't passed your Theory/ Practical tests before the two years are up, you will need to retake CBT in order to keep riding.

If you're happy to ride a 125cc bike with L-plates, there's nothing to stop you simply retaking CBT every two years, and never take the Theory/ Practical tests. Many car licence holders do this, as it enables them to ride a 125 for commuting to work, without taking the tests.

Theory test

The motorcycle test is far more stringent than it used to be, and consists of two parts – Theory and Practical. You must pass the Theory test before you can take the Practical. The Theory itself consists of two parts – multiple choice and hazard perception, both done on-screen. There are 50 multiple choice questions, and you have 57 minutes to complete them. Some need you to select more than one answer, but if you've studied your *Highway Code*, none should prove difficult. You can practice at home on the MCIA's website for new riders – www.geton.co.uk.

After a rest of three minutes, the hazard perception test comes up. You are shown a series of visible clips, in which a potential hazard develops – you need to identify this using the computer mouse, and the earlier you spot it, the higher your score. One of the clips has more than one hazard. Again, you can practice this test at www.geton.co.uk.

Practical test

Like the Theory test, the Practical comes in two parts. As with CBT, you

The Practical test also involves riding in and out of cones. (DSA Crown Copyright)

The on-road section of the Practical test allows the examiner to observe your riding. (DSA Crown Copyright)

must wear suitable gear or the test could be cancelled. The first part takes place at an official test centre, away from the road, where the examiner will watch you do the following:

• Place your bike on and off the stand
• Control the bike when pushing it
• The slalom (riding through five cones in a row)
• The figure of eight (riding around two cones)
• Circuit rides
• Hazard avoidance
• Controlled stops
• The U-turn
• Control at low speed
• The emergency stop

If you pass this first part, the examiner takes you out on the road on a pre-arranged route. He or she will be following you on a bike, watching your riding. If all of this sounds daunting then don't worry – your trainer will have taken you through every manoevre you will face on the test, and will only put you in for the test once s/he is convinced you're good enough to pass.

After the on-road test, the examiner will take you back to the test centre, and give you feedback on your test.

Further training

If you've passed your CBT, Theory and Practical tests, congratulations! But that's not the end of your training. In fact, it should never end for as long as you ride a bike. Packages of further training are available – everything from an hour-long observed ride to a complete Advanced Rider course and test, which will enable you to build on your skills and experience, becoming a safer rider. As well as taking advanced training, you can treat every ride as a learning experience, by being aware of what's going on and what action you need to take to stay safe.

Get On
If you're not sure about taking the first step toward getting your bike licence, then have a look at the Get On scheme. This is run by the Motorcycle Industry Association, and offers first-time riders a free try-out session, with no obligation to take it any further: www.geton.co.uk

Riding with a disability
Many people with a disability ride motorcycles, three-wheeler trikes, or sidecar outfits. If you want to find out more, the National Association for Bikers with a Disability is a good place to start. This voluntary organisation will be able to give advice on how you might start riding, and what modifications to the bike, if any, could make this possible. www.nabd.org.uk

John Liddiard has one arm, and passed his bike test.
(Courtesy NABD)

two

Documents you will need

To be legal on the road, you'll need four documents (five if your bike is over three years old): licence, V5C, insurance, tax disc, and MoT. There's no legal requirement to carry these with (except the tax disc, which must be displayed on the bike), but it's a good idea to always have your licence with you, at least.

Licence

A motorcycle licence looks exactly the same as the car photocard licence, except that the class of motorcycle you're entitled to ride (A, A1 or A2) is listed on front and back. You'll need to update it with a new photo every ten years – heartless, aren't they?

V5C

This the registration document for the

V5C registration document lists the bike's registered keeper.

Section 4 – Vehicle details, Section 5 – Registered keeper's details, Section 7 – Register any major changes to the bike here, Section 8 – Buyer and seller must sign this section when the bike is sold, Section 9 – Use this section when selling to a dealer, Section 10 – Kept by new keeper until new V5C arrives from DVLA, Section 11 – Use this section if exporting the bike.

bike, something you must complete and send off to DVLA Swansea as soon as you buy a bike, whether new or secondhand. DVLA will duly return it with your name and address included as the bike's registered keeper. Note the word 'keeper' – the V5C is not proof of legal ownership, just of who looks after the bike and takes the responsibility for registering and taxing it. But it's still an important piece of paper, which does show that your bike is registered and legal to use on the road.

Insurance

Insurance is absolutely essential, and would be even if it wasn't a legal requirement. Accidents can happen, and regardless of who's at fault, an insurance policy will protect you from the expenses and claims that can result.

As with car insurance, there are three basic types of policy – Third Party Only, Third Party, Fire & Theft, and Comprehensive. Third Party Only is the basic legal requirement, and only protects you against claims from another person (the 'third party') – it won't cover your bike if it's damaged or stolen. This basic policy is rarely available in practice. Third Party Fire & Theft is a step up, covering your bike if it's stolen or suffers fire damage, plus usually any injuries to a pillion passenger.

Comprehensive is the ultimate, covering any damage to your bike (even if the crash was deemed to be your fault) as well as everything else listed above.

Insurance premiums can come as a shock, though the actual price you pay is affected by many factors. Some of these – age, sex (female riders often pay less, as they're a better risk) and where you live – you have no control over, but some you do, as follows:

• Shop around. It takes time, but get quotes from a range of companies –

Insurers like to see bikes kept in a secure garage.

---

bennetts Insurance Certificate

Important:
1. A new certificate must be obtained before:
   (a) Any change of vehicle (b) Any change in Use or Driving
2. Any termination of the Insurance, which the Company may on request agree, will operate from the return of this certificate.

Advice to Third Parties:
Nothing contained in this Certificate affects your right as a Third Party to make a claim.

CERTIFICATE OF MOTOR INSURANCE

Certificate No.:   Insurer ref.: 32956846

1. Registration mark of vehicle
2. Policyholder
3. Effective Date of the commencement of insurance for the purpose of the relevant law:
   12.01 hours on the 8th March,2012
4. Date of Expiry   12.00 hours on the 8th March,2013

5. **Persons or classes of persons entitled to drive:**
As defined below provided that the person driving holds a licence to drive the vehicle or has held and is not disqualified from holding or obtaining such a licence.
The Policyholder

The policyholder is also insured to ride with the owner's consent any motorcycle not belonging to him/her and not hired to him/her under a hire purchase or lease agreement and provided that the motorcycle is being used within the limitations listed below. This cover is restricted to Third Party Liability only. Excluding use to secure the release of a motor vehicle(s), other than the vehicle(s) identified above by its registration mark, which has been seized by, or on behalf of, any government or public authority.

6. **Limitations as to use:**

• Use for social, domestic and pleasure purposes including commuting

Exclusions
• Despatch, courier and messenger services, or food delivery. Racing, pacemaking or being in any contest or speed trial (road safety rallies and treasure hunts will be covered).
• Riding on any race track or circuit or de-restricted toll roads or the Nurburgring Nordschleife.
• Trials (apart from where **your motorcycle** is travelling on a road which the public have access to).
• Hiring – letting out **your motorcycle** for a sum of money.

I hereby certify that the Policy to which this Certificate relates satisfies the requirements of the relevant law applicable in Great Britain, Northern Ireland, the Isle of Man, the island of Jersey, the island of Guernsey, the island of Alderney.
For and on behalf of
Equity Red Star
Authorised Insurers

Equity Red Star

Mark Bacon
Underwriter

For full details of the insurance cover reference should be made to the policy.

Policy Schedule bennetts

SCHEDULE FORMING PART OF THIS INSURANCE

Reason for Issue: Renewal   Date Issued: 05/03/2012

Name: Address:

Policy Number: Insurer ref: 32956846

Operative from: 8th March,2012   12.01 hours   Cover is only valid if your
                                                  premium payments are up to date
Expiry date: 8th March,2013   12.00 hours

Occupation:

Make: DUCATI   Model: ST4   c.c. 916

Value: £2500   Year: 1999   Reg No:

Authorised Driver(s) and Limitations as to Use:
As specified in the current Certificate of Motor Insurance under this policy but subject to any restrictions imposed by this policy.

Cover: Comprehensive

Optional Extra Cover: Renewal: £116.18
None selected
                                         TOTAL = GBP 116.18

Excess Details: Voluntary   £400
                           Compulsory   £250   (including a renewal arrangement fee and insurance
                                                 Premium Tax where applicable)
Your bank account details will be kept on our records so we can automatically process any changes you make and renew your policy.
If you do not wish this account to be used for future payments call Customer Services on 0844 412 2171.

Endorsements applicable:
For full details of any policy endorsements, please see overleaf.

Equity Red Star is managed by Equity Syndicate Management Limited which is authorised and regulated by the Financial Services Authority.
Equity Syndicate Management Limited is Registered in England no. 426475.
Registered Office: Library House, New Road, Brentwood, Essex CM14 4GD

Typical insurance certificate. Read the Limitations and Exclusions very carefully.

some will reduce their premiums to make them competitive. But do check that you're comparing like with like, as policy small-print can vary.

• Keep the bike locked away. Insurers love to see bikes locked up in a secure garage. Locked up on your drive (ie off the road) is the next best thing.

• Get some more training. Recognised advanced riding courses, run under the Driving Standards Agency's Enhanced Rider Scheme, or the IAM or ROSPA courses, should get you a discount. Of course, with advanced riding skills under your belt, you're less likely to have an accident in the first place.

• Limit your mileage. Some policies offer lower premiums if you can limit your riding to, say, 3000 miles a year. Probably not applicable if you're planning to use the bike every day, but worth working out your mileage otherwise.

• Modifications. Check with the insurer first if you're thinking about modifying your bike. An aftermarket exhaust is easy to fit, but could increase the premium. If you don't tell the insurer, your policy will be invalid.

There's one more thing to add on insurance. However tempting it is to 'underestimate' your mileage or invent a fictitious bricks-and-mortar garage, don't do it. If you make a claim, any false statements will inevitably be found out, giving the insurance company the perfect excuse not to pay you anything at all.

Read the exclusions and limitations sections of your insurance document very carefully.

Tax disc

Officially known as the Road Fund Licence, this is the familiar tax disc which must be displayed by all road registered vehicles. As with a car, you can buy or renew a tax disc at most Post Offices. Tax disc renewal is used as an official check that you have insurance, MoT, and that the bike is registered in your name, so the Post Office counter person will want to see both insurance and MoT certificates and the V5C before handing over your nice new tax disc.

In its wisdom, the Department for Transport still charges for the tax disc on small motorcycles, despite giving free tax discs to small cars with low CO_2 emissions. Still, that's the world we live in, and bigger bikes (over 600cc)

You'll get a reminder when the tax disc needs to be renewed.

do pay less road tax than family cars. If you are one of the few people to ride an electric motorcycle, your tax disc is free. It's also free if your bike was first registered before 1st January 1973, but in both cases, you will still need to display the free tax disc, and renew it each year.

When your tax disc is due for renewal, DVLA will send a reminder. If you decide not to retax it because you're not intending to use the bike for a while (some riders do this over the winter) then you must tell the DVLA. This is called SORN (Statutory Off Road Notification) and you just need to fill in the relevant part of the renewal reminder form.

MoT

Just like a car, any motorcycle over three years old must have a current MoT certificate to be road legal. The MoT is a safety check, showing that items like brakes, tyres, lights, were all working correctly on the day of the test, and that the bike was in a roadworthy condition. It's no guarantee that a bike is still roadworthy for the entire 12 months the certificate is valid for, so it's still the rider's responsibility that the bike is maintained in a roadworthy condition. If you own an old bike, built before 1st January 1960, it does not need an MoT test, but if it's found to be unroadworthy, say after a police spot check, then you'll be in trouble. This legislation came into force in November 2012 – prior to that, even pre-1960 bikes had to have an MoT.

Unlike the tax disc, you won't get a renewal reminder for the MoT, so it's worth keeping in mind when this is coming up. Do book the MoT for a couple of weeks before it runs out – that way, you'll have time to get the bike put right and retested if that's needed. If the bike doesn't have an MoT, or fails the test, you are still allowed to ride it on the road, but only in the following circumstances: to the MoT station for a pre-booked test; from the MoT station to a place of repair (if it fails); and to/from a place of repair if the repair has been pre-booked.

An MoT test is needed every 12 months for bikes over three years old.

three
Clothing & kit

Buying the proper gear to go with your bike – helmet, gloves, jacket, trousers, boots – should keep you warm, dry and far better protected than you would be with just normal clothes. Added up, this lot won't be cheap, but nor will they (excuse the pun) cost an arm and a leg. Considering what they are protecting, they're well worth the money.

Helmet

A good quality helmet could save your life, so it pays to spend as much as you can afford – it is the most important piece of riding kit you will buy. All helmets have to meet minimum safety standards, but the Department for Transport also tests every helmet and gives it a star rating, from one to five. On the website, (www.sharp.direct. gov.uk) you can search the ratings for helmets of a particular make, type or price range.

Of course, you could buy a secondhand helmet, and these do indeed make excellent flowerpots, but are useless as head protection. Always buy new.

Flip-up full-face helmet, flipped down ...

... and flipped up for fresh air.

Open-face helmets offer the ultimate in fresh air, but this Schuberth has a chin guard to improve crash protection.

Most modern helmets are full-face, though open-face are increasingly popular amongst cruiser and scooter riders. Full-face obviously gives more protection, though a few open-face helmets incorporate an unobtrusive chin guard which increases protection while keeping that wind in the face feeling. A full-face helmet can also feel claustrophic, especially in traffic, and one compromise is the flip-up, a full-face on which the chin guard can be hinged up and out of the way when stationary.

The fit of the helmet is crucial, as a loose-fitting helmet could actually get torn off your head on impact. Try on a few in the shop before buying. It shouldn't be tight across the forehead, but a good snug fit all around is fine – the lining will 'give' slightly as it gets used, and mould itself to your shape.

Look after your helmet. If it gets dropped onto a hard surface from more than a couple of feet, it should be replaced. Visors are often described as 'anti-scratch' but they still will, so clean with a sponge and warm soapy water. Store the helmet in a helmet bag, if you have one. Helmets should be replaced every five years or so

One thing you can't check in the shop is how much wind noise the helmet allows, though, as a rule, full-face helmets are the quietest. Eventually, prolonged exposure to wind noise will damage your hearing, so earplugs are a good idea. The cheapest solution are soft sponge plugs that you replace every now and then, up to custom-made silicon plugs that fit your ear shape exactly.

Gloves

If riding all year round, you'll need more than one pair of gloves, but to keep the cost down, buy a pair to suit the season you start riding in, then add

Lightweight leather glove with Gore-tex lining.

Warmer and roomier gauntlet for the winter.

more when you need to. Lightweight summer gloves should be leather for protection, though they won't be waterproof. All-season gloves should be leather or fabric with a breathable waterproof lining, and with thicker padding than the summer gloves. For riding in winter, you really want what used to be known as gauntlets, with a big opening to cover the jacket cuffs and keep out draughts.

Whatever you're buying, try them on in the shop – they shouldn't be tight or too bulky.

Jacket & trousers

There are two alternatives when it comes to jacket and trousers – leather or textile. Leather gives the best protection against abrasion, not to mention the classic 'biker' look and feel that lots of people fall in love with. Modern textiles are more practical all year round though, often lighter to wear, and usually have a breathable waterproof lining built in. You can, of course, carry a one-piece lightweight oversuit that slips over leathers if the heavens open. One-piece textile suits are bulky, but keep out the weather better than a separate jacket and trousers. One-piece leathers offer the ultimate crash protection, but they're not very practical off the bike.

Go for an established make, and

Modern fabric jackets with a breathable lining offer better weather protection than leather.

For some, leather is the only choice.

buy from a decent dealer rather than from a website – as with every other item of bike gear, you should try it on first, and many dealers now have clothing specialists to advise. With jackets, look for the official marking CE EN 13595, which shows that it has passed tests for abrasion, impact, cut and burst resistance. Zip covers will help prevent rain getting in. The jacket should be big enough to fit an extra layer underneath for when it's colder, though most of them also have a zip-out quilted lining.

Does the jacket or trousers have armour? This gives extra protection to the shoulders, elbows, knees or hips,

Leather lowers give great slide protection.

should be CE-approved, and also flexible enough that it doesn't restrict your movement. Does the jacket have back protection? Not all jackets do, and one alternative is a separate back protector than can be unclipped when you're off the bike.

If heavy armoured trousers feel too restrictive, armoured jeans are a good alternative. They don't offer the ultimate protection of leather, but with an abrasion resistant lining behind the denim, are a good compromise, and are lighter, cooler and easier to walk about in than full-scale motorcycle trousers.

Boots

Once again, leather offers the most protection, and many leather boots now

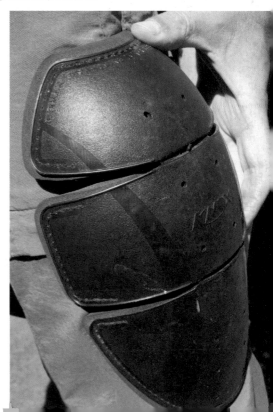

The best armour is flexible and lightweight.

have a breathable waterproof lining as well – if not, there are various waterproofing treatments on the market that will help keep water out, at least for a while.

A good motorcycle boot has a stiff, grippy sole (you don't want to lose your footing as you come to stop) and the CE marking to look for is EN13634, which shows that the boot is up to safety standards. The boot should cover your ankle – taller boots up to the knee give more protection, but are less easy to walk about in. Either way, they should be a snug fit so that they can't come off in an accident.

If you can't afford to buy proper motorcycle boots straightaway, then good quality walking boots, if you have them, if they have the ankle protection that motorcycle boots offer, are an acceptable stopgap, but do watch out for laces coming loose and dragging on the ground (or the loops catching on the footpeg when you go to place your foot on the ground).

Ahh, heated kit

The ultimate in luxury for cold weather riding is electrically heated riding kit. It's now relatively affordable as well, and is available as heated seats and handlebar grips. The heated seat is an option on a few top-range touring bikes, but heated grips are a very popular and affordable accessory. These will fit any bike, but, unless you're familiar with electrics, having them fitted may be your best option.

Armoured jeans are a good compromise between comfort and protection.

Even short bike boots will give good ankle and foot protection. (DSA Crown Copyright)

Heated grips mean warmer hands.

The other option is heated clothing, whether it's the gloves, jacket, trousers or even heated soles for boots. All of these work really well, the only drawback being the necessity for a lead between yourself and the bike, which must be disconnected when you get off. Power comes directly from the bike's own battery.

Wearing all this heated kit at once is a bit over the top, unless you're planning to ride a long way in sub zero temperatures. A good compromise is heated grips to keep your hands warm, plus a heated inner waistcoat, which keeps your core warm while avoiding the complication of multiple wires and connectors.

Heated waistcoat is plugged into the bike.

four
Typical control layout

Controls: 1. Throttle. 2. Engine kill switch. 3. Starter button. 4. Front brake lever. 5. Clutch lever. 6. Indicator switch. 7. Dip/main beam switch. 8. Horn. 9. Rev counter. 10. Speedometer. 11. Heated grip control (accessory).

five
Which bike?

Which bike you decide to buy depends on the sort of riding you want to do. And the choice you make matters, because motorcycles come in all shapes, sizes and characters. Think of the average car – it's got a four-cylinder engine, front-wheel drive, and most of them are hatchbacks. That's why car manufacturers spend so

Think about what you'll use the bike for. This is a Triumph Tiger adventure tourer.
(Courtesy Triumph Motorcycles)

A Harley Sportster can make a good, if heavy, first bike. (Courtesy Harley-Davidson)

much on advertising – they are trying to differentiate what are really very similar machines.

Modern motorcycles are extremely diverse. They may have one, two, three, four or six cylinders, and almost every type of engine layout under the sun – they come as sports bikes, adventure tourers or big scooters, all aimed at very different uses and riders. This diversity is partly what makes bikes so fascinating, but it also makes your choice of first bike more difficult.

You may love the look and aura of a Yamaha R1 sports bike, but you might well find it heavy, awkward in town, and uncomfortable over distance. It also has enough power to scare many riders (even some experienced ones) out of their riding wits. In fact, that's a good point to start with. Even if you can afford to buy a big bike straightaway as your first machine, don't do it. Big bikes have so much performance that they can

easily catch out inexperienced riders. Start on something more modest, build your skills and experience, then, when you feel ready, trade up.

Right, that's narrowed the choice a bit. Now, have a think about what you'll be using the bike for. If your immediate reaction is, "Just a bit of fun at weekends, sometimes with a passenger, and occasionally into work," then a naked bike is a good all-round compromise. On the other hand, if you have a more specific use in mind – a long distance tour, or year-round commuting, or to have a go at off-road riding – then a more specialised bike would suit you better.

As well as being fit for your purpose, the bike has to fit you. Cars might all be similar in a dull sort of way, but they do fit all shapes and sizes of people, with multi-adjustable seats and steering wheels to get the driving position just right. Motorcycles aren't

Bar risers will raise the handlebars by an inch or so.

like that – the riding positions vary a lot, and very few bikes offer much adjustment, so really the standard position has to be something you are comfortable with.

So, take your time in the showroom, and sit on a few different styles of bike before going for a test ride – a good salesman will understand, ask what you'll be using the bike for, and hopefully steer you towards the right choice. (Beware of the salesman who tries to talk you into a bigger/more expensive bike than you need). It will help to have riding gear on, as that gives a more realistic impression of what the bike will be like to sit on out on the road.

One more thing about fit – seat height. Don't expect to be able to get both feet flat on the floor while sitting on the bike (though this is possible on many cruisers), but if you can only reach the ground with one tiptoe, that won't give enough grip to keep the bike upright as you roll to a stop, especially if it's heavy. Worrying about a high seat can really affect your confidence at slow speed manoevring, so it's important that the seat is low enough for you to

feel in control. A few bikes do have height adjustable seats, and there are specialists around who will cut some foam out of the seat to make it lower.

Naked bike

Naked bikes, so called because they have no bodywork, are the great all-rounders. They are what used to be the standard roadster motorcycle, with no fairing, medium-height handlebars and an exposed engine. They come in all sizes, from 125cc commuters to 1000cc-plus muscle bikes, and what they offer is an undiluted motorcycling experience. For the experience of being out in the breeze, exposed to the elements, there's nothing quite like one of these, except for some cruisers.

The Triumph Bonneville is a retro-look naked bike. (Courtesy Triumph)

obvious example, and the Indian-made Royal Enfield Bullet another. If you like the idea of a classic bike, but with electric starting and modern reliability, then have a look at these.

Sports bike

Until recently, Britain's motorcycle culture was dominated by sports bikes, and they remain an important sector of the market. Sports bikes are highly focussed on just one thing – performance – with considerations like comfort and practicality coming second. They are the closest thing you can get to a racing bike on the road, and, in fact, most can take to the track with only minimal modifications.

Yamaha's R1 and R6 are typical performance-focussed sports bikes. (Courtesy Yamaha)

Royal Enfield Bullet gives something like a 1950s riding experience. (Courtesy Fabulous Biker Boys)

Because they are very much a basic motorcycle, naked bikes are cheaper than other types, and adaptable – it's often easier to fit luggage or other accessories to one of these, and some riders do add these things to make them suitable for touring or commuting. Also, the average age of riders is increasing, and a naked bike is the sort of machine many of them started out on. The Suzuki Bandit and Yamaha Fazer helped popularise this class, and many of these bikes are available secondhand.

A sub-group is retro bikes, which like certain cars are styled to evoke a bygone era. The Triumph Bonneville is the most

Riding a sports bike is an experience, and the lean-forward position never lets you forget it – the performance and handling are in a different world to most other vehicles on the road. Most are either 600cc 'supersports,' such as the very successful Honda CBR600, or 1000cc-plus (Honda FireBlade, Yamaha R1). Sports bikes look fearsome, but they are easier to ride than you might think, especially the 600s.

On the other hand, they do have several disadvantages. Insurance and running costs are high, and the riding position can be uncomfortable at lower speeds. Pillion accommodation is a bit of an afterthought, and luggage is limited to soft 'throwover' panniers. Some riders do tour on their sports bikes, but you have to be keen.

Sports tourers (this is a Triumph Sprint ST) offer fine performance and decent comfort. (Courtesy Triumph)

Sports tourer

The sports tourer is a sort of halfway house between a sports bike and a tourer, combining the best elements of both. The idea is to have a sporty riding position and fine performance/handling, but with more generous room for a pillion and provision for hard luggage.

The class was personified by the Honda VFR, and later by Triumph's Sprint ST. Both could tour reasonably comfortably two-up, cruise long distances on motorways, be fun to ride over mountain passes, and even tackle track days. Sports tourers are usually big-engined (at least 800cc) and are seen by some as the perfect compromise, though their popularity has waned in recent years as more riders opt for an adventure tourer.

A good first-bike choice is the Suzuki SV650S, which has been around for several years but is still in production – it handles very well, has a lovely V-twin engine, and is fast enough for any new rider. There are lots of these available secondhand.

Adventure tourer

Adventure tourers are really the two-wheeled equivalent of a Range Rover – a big, well-equipped machine with a suggestion of off-road ability. This bias towards muddy tracks and desert pistes is often nominal, though harder-edged adventure tourers, such as the KTM Adventure, really are capable of tackling the rough stuff, as long as the rider has skills to match.

The class was pioneered by BMW back in the 1980s with the R80G/S, a bike which has evolved into today's far more sophisticated, larger and heavier R1200GS, which remains the undisputed world leader in this class. BMW has Ewan McGregor and Charley Boorman to thank for that, in part – their televised round the world trip in

Adventure tourers like this Suzuki V-Strom are increasingly popular. (Courtesy Suzuki)

Typical trail bike, the Honda CRF250L. (Courtesy Honda)

Long Way Round did a huge amount to popularise this type of bike. So, although a growing number of people buy adventure tourers and really do big overland trips, many more like them for their rugged image.

Having said that, adventure tourers have many practical advantages. Most are very comfortable, thanks to long-travel suspension and a relaxed, upright riding position. There's plenty of room for two, and hard luggage is easy to fit. Adventure tourers also come in a wide range of sizes, from the 700cc Honda Transalp to the 1200cc Triumph Explorer.

Trail bike/enduro

If adventure tourers are the Range Rovers of motorcycling, then trail bikes and enduros are the short-wheelbase Land Rovers. These are geniune on/off road bikes, smaller and lighter than an adventure tourer, and often with a single-cylinder engine from 125 up to 600cc. Suzuki's DRZ 400 is typical, with the riding position, long-travel suspension, and knobbly tyres to cope with off-road riding. Bikes in this class often have a high seat, and are less sophisticated in feel to multi-cylinder road bikes.

There are various incarnations of the same basic type. The trail bike or 'traillie' is more road biased, and many of these are used purely on tarmac. They are less comfy than pure road bikes, but their light weight and slim dimensions make them popular for

Supermoto (Suzuki DRZ400) is a trail bike with road wheels and tyres. (Courtesy Suzuki)

urban riding, though knobbly tyres have less grip than standard road tyres. The enduro is more serious about its off-road abilities, which compromises its suitability for the road.

Another variation is the supermoto, which originated in France and is really a trail bike with smaller wheels and very grippy road tyres. These, combined with good brakes, light weight and wide handlebars, make supermotos ideal for wheelies and stoppies – of course, indulge in those on the road, and you'll soon get into trouble, but supermotos have a cult following of their own.

Tourer

Touring bikes are big, luxury machines, built to travel long distances in great comfort. Because of their size and weight, they're probably not the best choice of first bike, but if your ultimate aim is long distance rides, heading down to Spain or across to the Czech Republic or Greece for a few weeks, then it's something to graduate to when you are ready for a bigger bike.

Tourers usually come with a big 1000cc-plus engine, and are very well equipped, with items like ABS, cruise control, heated grips and hard luggage all standard. They are heavy with a long-wheelbase, so they don't handle as well as lighter bikes, but can be hussled along surprisingly quickly. Excellent weather protection from a large protective fairing and big screen is an essential element, as is shaft drive. There's a generous fuel tank to give big miles between fill-ups.

As in every other sector, there are different degrees of tourer. Yamaha's FJR1300 is at the sportier end of the spectrum, and Honda's unique six-cylinder Goldwing right at the other. Another Honda, the 700cc Deauville,

Yamaha FJR1300 is at the sportier end of the touring spectrum, but comfy all the same. (Courtesy Yamaha)

is the only mid-size tourer currently available – worth looking at if you want the weather protection and luggage, but in a smaller package.

Cruiser

Cruisers seem to encapsulate the American Dream, the summation of decades of Stateside popular culture that conjures up freedom, far horizons, and an endless, empty, two-lane blacktop. They're also big business, and the success of Harley-Davidson in pedalling this all-American lifestyle choice means that most major manufacturers build a cruiser of some sort.

Most of these take their inspiration from a Harley or Indian of the 1940s or '50s. The essential elements are a long-wheelbase, low seat, and high pulled-back bars. A big engine isn't mandatory (125cc cruiser-styled bikes are popular with learners) but most opt for a V-twin of at least 800cc, preferably a lot more. Triumph is an exception, in terms of engine layout, with the parallel-twin Thunderbird and Rocket III triple – the latter, at 2.3 litres, is the biggest-engined production bike in the world. Not recommended as your first bike!

There is something to be said for choosing a cruiser. A lot of new riders like the low seat and laid back, comfortable riding position. The engines are invariably forgiving, tuned for low-

Harley-Davidson encapsulates the cruiser image. (Courtesy Harley-Davidson)

and mid-range torque rather than top-end power, which makes these bikes easier to ride. On the other hand, most cruisers are big, heavy bikes, with very little on offer between the 125cc cruiser-style bikes, and the big 800cc-plus machines. One worth looking out for (only available secondhand now) is the Yamaha Dragstar 650, which was produced until recently. Harley's 'smallest' bike, the Sportster 883, is no lightweight, but some are bought as a first bike.

There are subtle variations within the cruiser genre – custom, bagger, tourer and muscle-cruiser – reflecting the fact that cruisers are really a world of their own.

Big 'scooters' & semi-automatics

This book is about motorcycles, not scooters, but the boundary between the two has blurred somewhat in recent years, thanks to the advent of bigger-engined scooters and semi-automatic bikes. If you don't want to be bothered by a clutch and gears, then there's a lot to be said for a big scooter, which will have a fully automatic 'twist-and-go' transmission.

Big scooters start with 300cc machines like the Vespa GTS (which looks just like a traditional scooter). Suzuki's 400cc Burgman is altogether bigger, with more room for two people and real touring potential. The 500cc Yamaha T-Max is the sportiest offering in this class, while Suzuki's 650cc Burgman is the biggest of all, with the added sophistication of a transmission that can switch between fully automatic and push-button gearchanging.

All of these (even the Vespa) will have no problem keeping up with motorway speeds, and all have built-in luggage space under the seat, plus

Honda Integra is a 700cc 'scooter.'
(Courtesy Honda)

Honda NC700 is offered with semi-automatic as well as manual gearbox. (Courtesy Honda)

far better weather protection than any motorcycle this side of a fully-faired tourer.

If you really can't contemplate a scooter, then there are a few motorcycles with the option of a clutch-free semi-automatic transmission. Most, like the Yamaha FJR1300 AS and Honda VFR1200, are big, heavy machines, but Honda's NC700 is the exception.

125cc

Now you might think that small 125cc bikes are not worth bothering with – fine for learning to ride on, but with none of the power and glamour of a big bike. The latter is certainly true, but, on the other hand, 125s do have their uses. The first and most obvious advantage is that you can ride one on a provisional motorcycle licence – you just need to take CBT, but you don't have take the full Theory and Practical tests. You will have to retake CBT every two years, keep L-plates, and take no passengers, but riding a 125 this way is the cheapest and simplest route to owning a bike.

Modern 125s can keep up with the traffic, are able to top 65-70mph, so they won't be out of place on dual carriageways, though the outside lane of a motorway is asking a bit much. As you'd expect, they are also cheap to run, easier on consumables than big bikes, with lower insurance premiums and lower fuel consumption than anything else on the road this side of a bicycle – expect 100mpg or more.

There are also plenty to choose from, with cheaper Chinese-built bikes as well as a whole variety of models from the big Japanese names, including trail bikes (eg Yamaha's WR125), cruisers (Suzuki's Marauder), sports bikes (Honda's CBR125R), and even adventure tourers (Honda's Varadero).

There are a couple of disadvantages, though. If you pass your test and need to take a passenger, then the extra weight will put a serious dent in the average 125's

A 125cc bike has plenty of performance for urban riding. (Courtesy Honda)

footer would feel cramped. Otherwise, for commuting, or even lower speed touring, they make for a great introduction to biking.

Narrow it down

Once you've decided on the type of bike that will suit you best, try to narrow it down to two or three models. Ask a dealer's advice and have a look at the owners' online forums (though these aren't always reliable). Once you've done all that, get insurance quotes for the models on your shortlist – there's no point in going to look at bikes which turn out to need a second mortgage to insure.

performance. Also, most of these bikes are physically small, so a six-

125s can do long distance, too! This Lexmoto did Bristol to Glasgow in a day, at 128mpg!

six

The buying process

Let's assume you're buying a used bike – buying new makes life much easier – just visit the nearest dealership selling the make of bike you're interested in and take it from there. However, many of us can't afford to buy a new bike, at least first-time round, so the next section assumes it's a secondhand sale.

First of all, do some research on the sort of prices you can expect to see. Check eBay (the 'Buy it Now' prices rather than low initial bids) and the relevant websites for *MCN, Bike Mart, Autotrader* and others – all show bikes for sale and their asking prices. Look at dealer prices as well as the private classified ads. You'll soon get a feel for the going rate for the bike you are interested in, or, if you've got a fixed budget, what it will stretch to.

Buying from a private seller

Inevitably, some bikes will come up

at dealerships, others will be sold privately. A private deal should prove cheaper than a dealer, and being open to private sellers does give you more choice, but there are a few things to bear in mind. Private sellers have far fewer legal obligations than do traders. There's no warranty, and their only obligations are that the bike must match their description, and that it must be theirs to sell. If the worst happens and the bike does turn out to be a dud, you can resort to the courts, but this is more difficult than with an established business.

Because private sellers have fewer obligations, some less scrupulous dealers try to pass themselves off as private. There are some clues to look for. Be suspicious if you see the same phone number in several classified ads for different bikes, or if the seller's name doesn't appear on the V5C document as the last registered keeper. When you first phone up, ask if 'the bike' is still for sale – if the seller asks 'which one?' he could well be a dealer. If you think the 'private' seller really is a dealer, you can report this to the Citizens Advice Bureau (CAB) consumer service (www. adviceguide.org.uk).

However, let's not get this out of proportion – thousands of private deals are done every week without a problem, and most private sellers are genuine people, simply trying to get the best price they can.

Buying from a dealership

Buying from a dealership does give legal additional safeguards under the Sale and Supply of Goods Act. The bike must be of satisfactory quality, fit for purpose, and as described by the dealer. All of these are open to interpretation, but they give you a good basis for a legal claim if things go wrong. If the bike turns out not to be any of those, you have the right

Dealers have a reputation to protect, and the longer they've been in business, the better for you.

Franchise dealers have the best choice of a particular make.

to a repair, replacement or refund. Dealerships cannot legally have a 'sold as seen' or 'no refunds' policy. If they try to impose these, you can report them to the CAB, as detailed above.

However, as with private sellers, most dealers aren't crooks. They have a reputation to protect, and the longer they've been in business on the same premises, the better a bet they are. Another advantage of dealerships is that they offer a lot more choice – you might be able to inspect several bikes in a single visit, rather than the one that a private seller has. Mind you, before the salesman drags bikes out of the showroom and starts them up for you, he will want to know you are serious about buying.

Should you go to an independent dealership, or one with a franchise for the make of bike you're interested in? Being open to independents gives more choice, and there's more likely to be

one local to you. Franchise dealerships tend to be more expensive, but they are more likely to have what you want, and some manufacturers run a 'used approved' scheme, which brings a warranty with it. The gold standard is to find a bike which the franchise dealership sold new and has done all the servicing. This is the most expensive way to buy, but probably the safest.

Online auctions

These days of course, many bikes are bought and sold online, using auction sites such as eBay. These, too, have a mix of private sellers and dealerships. If you do use an online auction site, check that there is a seller's history rating, and steer clear of sellers with a poor rating – there are plenty of good ones. Many bikes on sale via eBay and similar sites

Dealers offer more choice than private sellers.

are offered for fixed prices, so these ads can be treated as a normal classified – you're less likely to find a real bargain, but at least the price is predictable.

Whether the bike is being auctioned or sold for a fixed price, do go and view it before bidding or making an offer – the entry will show how far it is from your address, which is handy. Be aware that some machines offered on online auctions are 'ghost' bikes that don't exist or aren't really for sale, so don't part with any cash unless you're sure the bike does actually exist and is as described.

Traditional auctions are not a good way of buying your first bike. It's true that prices can be lower than either dealerships or private sellers, but it's not like buying from a dealership. The seller can legitimately label the bike as 'sold as seen.' It's also easy to get caught up in the adrenalin of the bidding process and pay more than you intended.

Find out as much as you can on the phone.

Phone checks

Whoever you buy from – dealership, private or online – find out as much as you can about the bike when you make that first phonecall. Ask about the mileage, the number of owners the bike has had, when the MoT and road tax expire, when it was last serviced, any modifications, and (if it's a private seller), why it's being sold. If the seller seems unsure about any of this information, or is reluctant to give much away, look elsewhere – there are plenty of legitimate bikes for sale.

There are other phone checks you can do before going to see the bike – it might still have finance owing, or have been written-off and rebuilt in a previous life. Various companies, such as HPI, and the RAC, can supply this information for a fee, given the bike's registration number.

Finance

Can you afford to buy the bike – whether new or used – outright? If so, you're in a good position. Offering a dealer cash rather than credit could induce him to reduce the price, and all credit (apart from 0 per cent finance deals) will end up costing you more in the long run.

It's more likely, though, especially for a new bike, that you will need to borrow money to close the deal. There are innumerable routes to cash loans, and there isn't the space here to go through even a fraction of them, but, in general, a traditional loan from a High Street bank or building society, or an online provider, is the most expensive way to go about it.

When comparing loans, always look for the APR percentage, which is effectively the 'price' of the loan. Check

Finance is tempting, but check you can see the commitment through to the end.
(Courtesy Black Horse)

the small print – there may be penalties if you try to pay off the loan early, and you don't want the loan company to repossess the bike for non-payment if you've paid off 90 per cent of it.

Bike dealerships will often be able to offer finance themselves. Franchise dealerships will have certain offers on certain bikes, such as low deposits or low interest (even 0 per cent interest) – these are often only available for limited periods. Other dealerships will offer finance through one of the established credit companies, such as Black Horse in the UK, and will be able to arrange everything in the showroom – as ever, check the APR and the small print, but this is a very convenient route to finance.

A more recent route is the PCP,

or Personal Contract Plan, which applies mainly to new bikes, though it can be offered on more recent used bikes as well. Instead of borrowing a lump of money to buy the bike, you effectively hire it for a fixed period, usually three years. This also gives the bike a Guaranteed Future Value, which it will be worth at the end of the period. When the three years are up you have three options: hand the bike back to the dealer with no more to pay; pay the Guaranteed Future Value (buying the bike outright); or swap it for a new bike and start again with another PCP deal.

PCPs are great for dealerships, because the customer has to come back to them, with an incentive to buy another bike. For buyers, PCP offers the prospect of a more expensive bike than you could otherwise afford, but the APR works out higher, and you will still need to make a deposit.

Warranty

If buying new, you will, of course, have a decent warranty, usually two years, which will give peace of mind. The downside is that this does tie you in to franchise dealership servicing for the period of the warranty. You may want to do that anyway (and you should get good service) but franchise dealership servicing is often more expensive than taking the bike to an independent.

If buying a used bike, the warranty is another good reason to buy from a dealer, as there's no such thing as a warranty from a private seller. If the bike is less than two years old, there may still be some manufacturer's warranty left to run, and this is transferrable to you as the new owner. The dealer may offer to sell you a warranty, but it's far better to have something included in the price, even if it's just for three months.

Typical finance deal summary sheet.
(Courtesy Black Horse)

If a warranty is part of the deal, check a few basic facts before signing up. It won't cover consumable items (tyres, chains, brake pads, etc) but should cover parts and labour (not just parts) if any faults come up. It might tie you into having the bike serviced at the dealership, and, if you modify the bike, or take it on a track day or go racing, the warranty will almost certainly cease to be valid.

seven
Examining the bike

If you're buying a new bike, you can skip this chapter because it's all about what to look for when buying secondhand.

If you aren't familiar with bikes, it's always best to take along a friend who is.

Let's assume you've arrived at the seller's house, or the dealership, to look at a specific bike – what next?

Documentation

The first thing to look at is the V5C

Ask to see all of the bike's documentation.

VIN plate is usually attached to the frame.

registration document. The person listed on the V5 isn't necessarily the legal owner, but their details should match those of whoever is selling the bike. The V5C will also list the VIN (vehicle identification number), which is unique to the bike – check that the VIN on the document matches that on the bike. The VIN is stamped on a plate which is usually located somewhere on the frame, often around the headstock, or stamped into the metal of the frame itself. If the numbers don't tally, or look as if they've been tampered with, walk away.

The MoT certificate is handy proof not just that the bike was roadworthy when tested, but a whole sheaf of them will give evidence of the bike's history – when it was actively being used, and what the mileage was. The more of these come with the bike, the better.

VIN number may also be stamped into the headstock.

Don't forget to check the mileage.

Ask for any service history paperwork as well – routine servicing, repairs and recalls.

Check the mileage – does it tally with the documentation and the bike's overall condition? Don't forget that bikes tend to cover fewer miles than cars – 40,000 miles is quite low for, say, a five-year-old car, but high for a bike. If it's been looked after, the bike should be fine at that mileage, but as there will be plenty of lower mileage examples around, the higher miles should be reflected in the price.

General condition

With the bike outside in good light, and on the centre stand if it has one, take a good, slow walk around it. Does it look tatty and neglected? Shiny on the bits you can see, but still shabby in nooks and crannies? Most bikes are given a smarten up to sell, and this can be very superficial. A generally faded look all over isn't necessarily a bad thing – it suggests a machine that hasn't been restored, and isn't trying to pretend that it has.

One crucial thing to look for is evidence of crash damage. Is the bodywork unmarked, or suspiciously new on an otherwise tatty bike? When a bike does hit the ground, the same things suffer almost every time, so take a good look at the silencer, footrests, mirrors, indicators, levers, and the tips

First, take a good general look around the bike.

of the handlebars for signs of trips down the road. Plastic bodywork protectors can be bent or scratched (though they're very easy to replace). Scraped engine or clutch cases (or even worse, holed cases, patched up with resin) are confirmation of a hard life. Holed cases apart, this may just be cosmetic damage, and underneath may be a perfectly fine motorcycle, but the price should reflect any scrapes, dents and bends.

For further evidence of crash damage, look closely at the steering stops (the little cubes of metal that prevent the handlebars from turning beyond full lock). If either is bent, then the bike has probably been crashed. While in this area, have a look around the headstock – flaking paint here is sign of a front end impact. If the seller doesn't have convincing explanation for any signs of damage, and you are in any doubt, walk away.

Rear wheel bearing check.

Check tyre condition, and the price of a new set, if necessary.

Check swingarm bearings for play.

49

Static checks

Have a look at the tyres; they're good indicators of whether or not the owner is a caring type. Are they worn right round to the sidewalls, or just in the centre? Worn tyres are a good bargaining point – find out the cost of a pair, so you can quote this to the seller.

Grasp the rear tyre (one hand at 9 o'clock; the other at 3 o'clock), and try rocking the wheel from side to side – if there's any movement at all, the wheel bearings need replacing. Grasp the swingarm and check that for side play as well – there should be none. While down at the rear of the bike, check the chain and rear sprocket – the chain should be properly tensioned and lubed. To check it for wear, try lifting it away from the sprocket – it shouldn't move

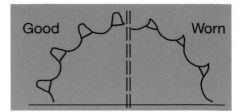

Chain drive bikes only. Check for worn sprocket teeth (they'll appear 'curved'). This may be more noticeable on the front sprocket.

far, and the sprocket teeth should be straight, not hooked.

Go to the front of the bike and do the wheel bearing check there, though it's trickier to do, because of steering movement. With the front wheel off the ground (only possible with a centre stand) get hold of the bottom of the fork legs and try rocking them backwards and forwards. Any play could be in the forks themselves, or the steering head bearings. Putting any of this right is a dealer job, so unless the seller is prepared to knock enough off the price to cover the cost, look elsewhere.

Now take the bike off the stand, and before you climb on board, push it a couple of feet backwards and forwards. It should move freely – if it feels reluctant, the brakes could be dragging, due to sticking calipers, something that's quite common if the bike hasn't been used for some time. With the front brake held on, push the forks up and down – they should move smoothly and easily, with no 'clonks.' Likewise, the rear shock, which should move smoothly and quietly: many cruisers and retro style bikes have twin shocks.

Put the bike back on its centre stand (or have someone support the bike vertically) and check the oil, either via a small dipstick or a little glass window at the bottom of the engine, usually on the right-hand side. If it's up to the right level, all well and good, but

Front wheel bearing check.

Front fork check.

Check the rear shock absorber for leaks and smooth operation.

Check the engine oil – is it properly topped-up and looking fresh?

ask when it was last changed. The bike will need to be upright (not leaning on the sidestand) for an accurate reading.

Now start-up – it's best if you can do this with the engine cold, as any nasty noises are more noticeable then. The engine should fire up promptly with the oil and charging lights (if fitted) going out immediately. Blip the throttle – the engine should rev up crisp and clean – but watch for blue smoke, a sign of top end wear. Listen to the sound of the engine – this is something that really needs experience, but modern engines are fairly quiet mechanically, so any untoward noise should be obvious. Most riders don't cover high mileages, so unless the bike has been badly neglected serious engine wear in modern bikes is relatively rare.

Test ride

Ideally, you (or your knowledgeable friend) will take a test ride. This is no problem at a dealership, which should also have insurance to cover prospective customers. You may have to sign a damage waiver form, which will certainly be the case with a new demo bike. Private sellers shouldn't be reluctant to allow a test ride, as it goes with the territory of selling a bike, but as long as you leave something behind (the vehicle you arrived in/on will do) then all should be well. Take your licence, in case they want to see it, and don't forget that you must be insured.

On the test ride, allow yourself a couple of minutes to familiarise yourself with the way the bike feels before thinking about its condition. It will inevitably feel odd at first, if you've not ridden this particular model before.

When you get going, change up through all the gears. The engine should pull cleanly and without hesitation from low to mediurm revs, though, of course, different engines have different characteristics, and some will be happier to do this than others. When you use the brakes coming up to a bend or a junction, the hand and foot lever travel should be slight, and they should slow the bike in a controlled manner. If the bike feels vague in corners, check the condition of the tyres (and tyre pressures) when you get back.

Back at base, check that the engine has settled back to a steady idle before switching off.

Find out as much as you can on the test ride.

Doing a deal

Some people don't like bargaining, or simply won't budge on the asking price, but many sellers will be flexible if they can see that you're serious and that a sale isn't far off. Think about any faults you've found and how much they might cost to put right – it's worth knowing roughly how much a new set of tyres, or chain and sprockets, or brake pads, will cost to buy and have fitted. You can then justify a lower price to the seller. If you really can't come to an agreement, then thank the seller for his/her time, and walk away – there are plenty of good bikes for sale.

If you do agree a price, private sellers of cheaper bikes will often prefer cash. You don't have to carry all this with you on the day, but take enough for a decent deposit so that the seller will hold the bike for you. If you're paying by cheque, you'll have to wait for it to clear before you can take the bike away. A banker's draft (a cheque issued by a bank) is as good as cash, but safer, so contact your own bank and become familiar with the procedure to obtain one. The quickest way of all to pay, if you're buying from a dealer, is with a debit/credit card, but only if you've got all the funds in place.

A dealer will give you a receipt, and a private seller should too, if you ask for one. The other essential piece of paperwork is the V5C registration document, which must be sent off to DVLA to notify it the bike has a new keeper. You'll need to fill in the green section 6 of the form, and both you and the seller must sign and date section 8, declaring that the bike has been sold. The seller must give you section 10 to keep (fill this in as well) and send the rest of the form to DVLA, who will duly send a new V5C to you, with your details included as the registered keeper.

Most sellers, whether private or dealer, will be willing to haggle.

Getting it home

Getting the bike home may need thought if you haven't passed your test yet, or don't have insurance worked out. A dealership, as long as it's local, will probably deliver it for you, and make a long-distance delivery for an extra fee. Private sellers may not have the facilities to do this. Once you've paid for the bike and the V5C has been sent off, it's effectively your property and your responsibility.

The dealer will give you a receipt.

eight

Looking after your bike

Keeping it safe

When you've got the bike home, you'll naturally want to keep it secure. A locked-up garage is the best option, followed by being kept on your property out of sight. Parked on the drive, in sight of the road, is less safe, of course, and parked on the public road is the least secure option of all. However, bikes are stolen even from private garages adjoining a house, so it's a good idea to have extra security measures here too.

All new bikes are fitted with a steering lock, but that's not much of a deterrent. There's a wide range of aftermarket alarms and immobilisers available, though they usually need professional fitting. A good physical deterrent is something solid you can chain the bike to, and the best solution is a substantial ground anchor, which can be concreted into the garage floor or drive.

If you don't have a garage, but want

Chains are a good deterrent, though work best when attached to something solid, like a ground anchor.

to keep the bike under cover, there's at least one make of simple metal shed on the market, which is quite straightforward to bolt together, and will keep the bike dry and out of sight.

If there's really nowhere to keep the bike on your property, it will have to stay on the road, but this isn't as bad as it seems. A lot of bikes are kept on public roads all the time, and the secret seems to be a substantial chain or U-lock, plus a dull grey rain cover. The cover doesn't just keep the weather off, useful though that is, but makes the bike semi-invisible. As well as making it less of a

target for thieves, this puts off inquisitive young fingers.

When a bike is stolen, it's often broken up and the parts sold individuallly, as it's worth more that way and is less easily identifiable as a stolen machine. Various kits are available which can mark the bike's key components with a unique number that shows up in UV light. If the police are able to test suspect parts, they can examine them under UV and trace the original machine they came from. An alternative is the Datatag system, which attaches tiny electronic transponders to key components. Both systems are popular, and include unremovable stickers to warn thieves that the bike is protected.

One more thing about where to keep your bike. The other advantage

Tucked away in a locked garage is the most secure option.

A cover protects the bike from both weather and prying eyes.

of a garage or shed is that there's somewhere to keep your helmet and other kit, which takes up quite a lot of room – after a wet ride, better to let it dry out in the garage than have it cluttering up the hall.

Maintenance

You probably didn't buy your first bike in order to tinker with it, and most riders would rather use their bikes than take them to pieces. The good news is that modern motorcycles, like modern cars, need very little attention between services. Having said that, there are a few small jobs that will need doing at home, and which require very little mechanical ability. In any case, it's a good idea to just keep an eye on how your bike is running, even if it's not

due a dealer service for some time – motorcycle consumables (tyres, brake pads, etc) wear out more quickly on a bike than a car, and they might need replacing in the meantime.

There's another maintenance job that has nothing to do with mechanics – cleaning. Bikes are more difficult to clean than cars because of all the nooks and crannies, but it's an important job, because so much of the machine is exposed to wet, dirt and (worst of all in winter) road salt. If you neglect cleaning, the bike will end up looking shabby and be worth less when you come to sell it. Jet washing is the easiest method, but take care, as the powerful jet of water/detergent can work its way into electrical components (never aim it at the switchgear, for example), strip oil and grease from where they're needed (the chain and wheel bearings), and even remove chipped paint. Hand washing is safer!

Fluid levels

Fluid levels – engine oil, coolant and brake fluid – should be checked once a week. The exact procedure for all of these will be included in your bike's handbook.

Cleaning the bike can be rewarding.

Check oil sight glass with bike upright.

Brake fluid level sight glass.

Engine oil is checked either via a small dipstick or (more common now) a small glass window in the side of the crankcase, located low down, and usually on the right-hand side. Some bikes need to be checked with the engine cold, some after it has run for a few minutes – the handbook will tell all. The bike must be upright, not leaning on its sidestand, to give a true reading, so you may need a helper to hold the bike upright while you do the checking.

If there's a glass window, it should either be full of oil or at a level between the low and high marks. If the bike has a dipstick, unscrew it, wipe it clean and reinsert – it may need to be screwed all the way back in or just rested, but again the handbook will tell you. The oil level should be between the low and high marks.

If the oil needs topping up, locate the filler cap and add oil of the right grade – the handbook will specify what this is. Be careful, though, as it's easy to overfill, which is a tricky thing to put right (you'll have to remove the drain plug and let some oil out, which is awkard and messy) – topping up usually needs less oil than one thinks.

On some bikes engine oil level is checked via a dipstick.

The coolant level is easy to check, as the reservoir will be translucent, with low and high marks on the side. Some bikes should be checked on a cold engine, some with a warm engine – check the handbook. If the coolant needs topping up, use the correct ready-mixed coolant, not plain water, which will dilute the coolant and reduce its anti-freeze and anti-corrosion effectiveness.

The brake fluid level is easy to check, via a glass window in the side of the reservoir. The front brake reservoir is usually mounted on the handlebars, and the rear close to the rear brake pedal.

Chain lubrication/adjustment

Most bikes still use chain drive, which (let's be honest) is an antiquated system. The chain is exposed to water, grit and dirt, just as on vintage machines, so it wears relatively quickly, needing checking, lubrication, and sometimes adjustment at home in-between services. Of course, if your first bike has shaft or belt drive, then you don't need to bother with any of this and can pass smugly on to the next section.

Actually, modern O-ring chains with sealed-in lubricant have reduced the need for maintenance, and you could always have an automatic lubrication kit such as the Scottoiler fitted. But the fact remains that chains are not a fit and forget item, so here we go.

If your bike has only a sidestand (and many do, especially sports bikes) then the whole chain job will be far quicker and more convenient if you buy a paddock stand. These are steel frames that slot into the bike, and support the rear wheel off the ground.

First, check the chain tension. The exact amount varies from bike to bike,

Topping up engine oil is easy.

A paddock stand makes chain maintenance easier.

but 20-30mm of free play is usual. Move the bike forwards or back a few feet and check the tension again (or if you had the foresight to buy a paddock stand, spin the rear wheel by the same amount). Do this two or three times until you've checked the entire chain length. The reason for doing this is that chains do not wear at the same rate along their length, so you may find a tight spot – the tightest part of the chain is the one you should take the reading from.

If the chain needs tightening, loosen the rear axle nut, and turn the adjusters in the ends of the swingarm clockwise – the adjusters will be allen bolts or locknuts. The exact procedure will vary according to the bike, some have single-sided swingarms for example, so check the handbook. It's very important to turn the adjusters by equal amounts, or the rear wheel will be pulled out

of line – the best way is to count the flats on the allen key or the nut. Don't overtighten the chain, as this will put a strain on the gearbox bearings. Once you're happy with the tension, retighten the axle bolts, and check the chain tension again.

Chain lube comes in the form of an aerosol. Either spin the wheel or move the bike a little at a time to make sure the whole length of chain is covered. Apply the spray on the inside of the chain, as centrifugal force will do the rest of the job. If it's an O-ring chain, then the lube should be O-ring compatible. An O-ring chain seals the grease inside the chain rollers. It lasts much longer than a standard chain, but will still wear eventually, and still needs external lubrication and protection from moisture ingress. Most 600cc and bigger bikes have an O-ring chain.

Check tyre pressures often.

or rear helps) and check the whole circumference of the tyre for cuts or other damage. The minimum legal tread depth is 1.0mm, and if the tyre is worn below that in the centre, but you have plenty of tread on the sides, it will still be illegal. A big sports bike can get through a rear tyre in as little as 3000 miles, but most bikes, especially mid-size and smaller ones, can expect a tyre life of at least twice that. If you cover a lot of straight line miles, then the tyre will wear out in the centre first.

Tyre pressures are important too, and these can be checked with a gauge, just as on a car. Recommended pressures will be in the handbook, with a higher rear tyre pressure for two-up riding. It's sometimes tricky to fit the average garage airline onto a motorcycle tyre valve, if the valve is upright (not angled outwards), and brake discs get in the way.

Suspension adjustment

Many bikes, especially sports bikes, have fully adjustable suspension, so that spring rates and damping can be adjusted precisely, to suit the rider's weight and riding style. However, with your first bike a lot of these adjustments are needless complication. For much harder riding, and trackdays, in particular, front suspension adjustment can come into its own. Otherwise, it's best to leave everything on the standard setting.

The exception is rear suspension pre-load, which is well worth adjusting to take account of a pillion passenger and/or luggage. As it suggests, this pre-loads the spring, making it stiffer to cope with heavier loads. Some bikes have a remote adjuster knob, and more convenient still is BMW's ESA, which allows pushbutton adjustments from the

Brake pads and tyres

You may never need new brake pads between services but they're worth keeping an eye on. To check them, you'll need to peer through the gap in the caliper – it helps if you have a decent torch, even in daylight. Most brake pads have a wear indicator, a slot or line which should be visible. If it isn't, the pads may need replacing, so take the bike to your dealer for a check. New pads aren't expensive, and replacing them isn't a big job.

The tyres are obviously far more visible and easy to check. Spin the wheel (again, a paddock stand at front seat. More humble bikes need manual adjustment of the pre-load using a C-spanner, which is usually included in the toolkit. The handbook will tell you what to do, and the slotted adjuster is located at the top or bottom of the spring. The adjustment is usually in several steps, the lightest pre-load for a solo rider, the heaviest for two-up riding with luggage.

Rear suspension pre-load adjustment.

nine
Fitting accessories

For many riders, buying a bike is just the start, because the basic machine (tourers apart) will come without luggage, weather protection, or many other items that make life more convenient. There's a huge range of accessories out there to make your bike more comfy, better looking, better sounding, better protected ... the list is almost endless. As we haven't got room to go into them all, here are just a few of the more common items.

Carrying stuff

If bikes have a disadvantage, it's that most of them don't come with any means of carrying anything, apart from a tiny cubbyhole under the seat. Fortunately, there's plenty of luggage available, some of which can be ordered from new, and it splits into two basic types – soft, and hard.

Soft luggage is made of fabric or

Soft luggage is cheaper than hard, but less waterproof, and less secure.

plastic, is light weight, and is designed to be clipped on and off the bike quickly. It comes as a set of panniers, a tailpack (which sits on he rear half of the seat) or tankbag (which sits on top of the fuel tank). All are handy for bikes which

63

Aluminium panniers give the full 'Charley Boorman' look.

Tank bags attach by clips to a cover, or directly to a metal fuel tank by magnets.

won't accept hard luggage. Tankbags and tailpacks are especially useful (though you can't use a tailpack with a pillion) the former often able to convert into a rucksack for carrying off the bike.

Hard luggage is heavier and more expensive, and needs a rack permanently fitted to the bike first. It is more waterproof than soft luggage, though, more secure, and looks smarter. A topbox is cheaper than panniers and doesn't add to the bike's width, though it won't hold as much. If you want to emulate round the world motorcycle adventurers, go for one of the aluminium box sets.

Keeping comfy/protected

There are all sorts of ways to make a bike more comfortable – replacement seats are often an improvement on the plank-like items that some manufacturers fit. Screens, whether handlebar-mounted, or a taller version of the standard fairing screen, will do a better job of keeping the wind off. We've already mentioned heated kit, but heated grips deserve another few words, simply because they're so lovely to have in the winter. If you find the handlebars are too low and too far forward, a set of bar risers will bring them closer.

Keeping the bike protected is another avenue for accessories. If a bike is dropped, even at low speed or when stationary, a lot of damage can be done. Tubular steel crash bars will protect the engine cases, and nylon crash protectors or mushrooms will hopefully save the fairing from cracks and scrapes.

Aftermarket exhausts are another popular accessory, especially on sports bikes. These are often sold on liberating extra power, but often the difference is

A screen will make long rides less tiring, especially in winter.

marginal, and their real attraction is in making the bike sound and look different.

Does breakdown assistance class as an accessory? Whether it does or not, it's well worth having. New bikes will include this as part of the warranty, and some insurance policies make it part of the package as well. If you're not covered by either of those, there are plenty of breakdown packages available – they're not expensive for the peace of mind they give, especially if you're riding further afield.

ten
Where to go?

Places to see, people to meet

One of the best things about motorcycling is that you're never short of a destination, whether you want to meet up with other bikers or simply go for a ride on your own. Wherever you live in the UK, you won't be that far from an informal meeting place. It could be a seaside promenade, a local beauty spot, a greasy spoon cafe or a pub, but there will be somewhere. A common factor is that they are usually surrounded by decent roads, so that getting there and riding home is all part of the fun.

Every weekend, and often on a certain weekday night through the summer as well, bikes and riders will congregate. People go singly or in groups, and it's easy to get chatting, or just wander about, look at the bikes

Revived Ace Café on London's North Circular hosts dozens of events a year.

There's nothing like a bike rally – this is a Horizons Unlimited rally: a good place to meet overland travellers.

You meet the nicest people on a motorcycle.

Just you, the bike, and the open road ...

and soak up the atmosphere. Some of the best known biker meeting places are listed in the box out, but this is just a tiny fraction – there are countless other smaller venues.

All of these meets are informal, which is part of their attraction, but if you want something more organised, many dealers now arrange weekend rideouts for customers. Some manufacturers, keen on making buyers part of a big happy corporate family, run riders' clubs, of which Harley-Davidson's HOG is the best known, and probably the biggest. In fact, if you want to join a club, again there are plenty to choose from, from small local groups to national one-make clubs, like the Triumph, Honda or BMW clubs. The one-make clubs are great if

you are really keen on the model of bike you've ended up buying. There's a huge amount of knowledge and expertise around, and many club members will be only to glad to help you get the most out of your bike. Online forums focusing on a particular model do the same thing.

Organised shows are something else there's plenty of, whether your interest is in classic bikes, customs, or the latest machinery. National events like the National Motorcycle Show at the NEC, the Staffordshire Classic Bike Show, and the custom show at the Bulldog Bash are just the best known in their sector. There are plenty more – keep an eye on the magazines and websites for adverts.

If all this sounds a bit too 'bikey,'

Group riding is fun, but go at your own pace.

then there's a lot of pleasure to be had simply seeking out the best roads local to you. Start with a map, and look for the twistiest roads, especially those that head for higher ground or down to the sea. Don't restrict yourself to main roads, and you could find some fantastic routes not far from home that you didn't know were there. These are easily missed when you're driving a car and are simply focussed on getting from A to B. Some riders like to always have a destination, but there's also a lot to be said for setting aside a day, heading off and seeing where you end up.

A word about riding in groups. This can be a huge amount of fun, and there's nothing like cruising along with a group of friends, seeing one bike in front of you and another behind. But be cautious about riding with a group you

don't know, especially if they've got a tendency to crack on. If they do, and you're beginning to ride faster than you feel is comfortable, don't try to catch them up. Just carry on at your own pace, and you'll probably find them waiting for you at the next junction.

Through much of this book, we've assumed that you'll be riding solo, rather than carrying a passenger. If you have only just passed your test, build up some experience before taking a pillion – passengers (even the petite ones) add a fair bit of weight, and make the bike more difficult to control at low speeds.

Once you feel confident with a passenger, it really adds to the experience, and many partners enjoy riding pillion just as much as you do controlling the bike. Motorcycling is not, and never has been, a 'boys only'

Ace Café, London	http://www.ace-cafe-london.com
Box Hill, Surrey	.http://www.belm.org.uk
Devil's Bridge, Derbyshire	
Green Welly Stop, Perthshire, Scotland ..	http://www.thegreenwellystop.co.uk
Matlock Bridge, Derbyshire	
Poole Quay, Dorset (Tuesdays)	http://www.poolebikenight.net
Squires Café, West Yorkshire.	http://squires-cafe.co.uk
Weston Super Mare, Somerset (Wednesdays)	http://westonbikenight.rblr.co.uk

hobby, and at meets you'll see plenty of couples turn up together. And if we haven't made much mention of women riders, that's because women have always ridden bikes, always will, and a growing number are taking to it. Everything in this book applies to both sexes.

Go touring

These single days out are all very well, but it's nothing like actually going off touring by bike, whether it's a long weekend or a high-mileage fortnight. Several riders have even set off on major overland trips through Africa or South America on their first bike, but they are, needless to say, the exception. (In case you're wondering, they all got home safely).

If you do like the idea of touring, try a weekend in Britain first, and see how you get on. If you haven't done a long ride before, head for somewhere just a couple of hours from home on the first day, then venture a bit further on the second. Camping is the cheapest option and gives a certain freedom, though there's a lot more to carry on the bike, especially two-up. However you do it, taking off for a couple of nights away does add an extra dimension to the ride than simply knowing you're heading for home at the end of the day.

Let's assume that first weekend gives you a taste for touring. It'll probably be worthwhile sorting out

Overlooking the shores of Lake Garda, after a relaxed three-day ride from England.

some more permanent luggage for your bike – see earlier for the merits of hard and soft luggage, and once you've got luggage it makes the bike far more useable day-to-day, not just for holidays. When heading off for a higher

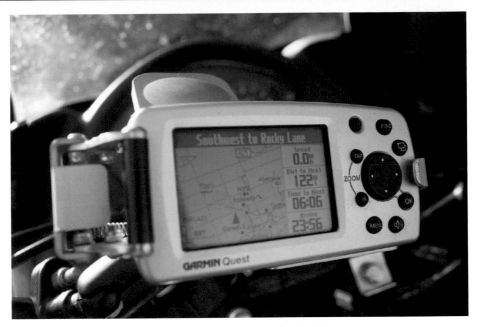

Weatherproof GPS units bolt to the handlebars.

mileage trip, do make sure your tyres and brake pads will last out, and that the bike won't be due a service before you get home. Of course, all of these things can be sorted while you're on the road, but it's far better to know that you won't need to bother with them.

The amount of planning you do, whether for route, accommodation or even destination, is entirely up to you. Some won't leave home unless every road and every night's bed is planned in advance – others like to plan nothing at all. It's always good to have some sort of loose plan, but if you are camping there's no need to book anything, unless you're heading for a tourist honeypot at the height of summer. As for finding your way, there are several bike-specific GPS units on the market now, which take a lot of the hassle out of route finding.

Crossing the English Channel, of course, opens up a whole new vista

of possibilities – riding down to the Mediterranean, over the Alps, or to the Italian Lakes or Greece. The European Union gets a bad press for many things, but one advantage of membership is that it makes travelling around this hugely varied continent much simpler than it used to be. The only essentials are to check that your insurance and breakdown assistance will cover you wherever you're going, and that you have an EHIC card, which entitles you to medical assistance in EU member states. You can apply for an EHIC online at www.nhs.uk, and it's free through that website – other sites may charge.

You might naturally feel nervous about heading abroad on your own for the first time, and a good introduction to the experience is an organised tour. Many companies now offer well organised trips to all parts of Europe, and one of the shorter ones – say a weekend in northern France – is a

71

good introduction to riding abroad. The company takes care of the ferry ticket and hotel booking, and recommends a route that you can either ride on your own or with the group. Some riders find they like this format so much that they stick with organised tours, year after year. Whatever works for you, works.

Advanced riding

Advanced riding is often taught in a group.

Passing the motorcycle test and tearing up those L plates is only the start of your development as a rider. One of the good things about biking is that riding skills are a constant learning curve – as your experience builds, you carry on learning. A lot of this happens just through practice, while riding on your own or with a group, but taking advanced rider training will give you a real insight into how to ride safely.

Advanced riding techniques have been around for decades, but getting extra training to acquire them is becoming increasingly popular, for some very good reasons. Advanced training will obviously reduce your chances of having a crash, whether self-inflicted or because of someone else's mistake. But there's a financial incentive too, as many insurance companies offer a discount if you've passed an advanced riding test: because they're less likely to come

to grief, advanced riders are a better risk. Also, because the whole ethos of advanced riding is based around smoothness, it should improve fuel consumption and reduce wear and tear on your bike – smoother riding means an easier life for brakes, tyres, chains and sprockets.

Advanced riding can be summed up in one word – anticipation. Some riders have a certain fatalism about accidents, but many crashes can be avoided simply by looking ahead far enough. The key to it is recognising potential hazards before they develop into something dangerous. In this way, you spot the car arriving at the junction slightly too fast well before it pulls out in front of you – it's all about planning and being prepared, rather than reacting.

Put like that, advanced riding sounds a bit dull, but putting it into practice actually adds to the fun. It's like having your eyes opened to the multiplicity of things that are happening all around you. After having advanced training, you'll never get bored on a bike.

Reflecting its increasing popularity, advanced rider training is available from many different sources, and if you don't want to take a test straight away, you don't have to. The RoSPA (Royal Society for the Prevention of Accidents) and IAM (Institute of Advanced Motorists) advanced tests have been around for many years, and are very well respected. Typically, you'll have an initial assessment ride, with an observer following you, with feedback on your strengths and weaknesses afterwards. You will have as many observed rides as they think are needed to get you up to advanced test standard. The IAM also offers RideCheck, which is a single, hour-long riding assessment – a good intial try-out of advanced riding. IAM's Road Rider Plus is aimed at 125cc

Buy your first bike, stay safe – and enjoy.

riders who have CBT but aren't planning to take the full motorcycle test – this half-day of training is well worth doing if you're aiming to commute by bike every day. All of this is conducted by a trainer local to you.

The Department of Transport's Driving Standards Agency is getting in on the act as well, with its Enhanced Rider Scheme, offered through independent trainers all over the country. There's no test, but you do have a one-to-one riding assessment with feedback. The DSA recomends you give this a try after passing the standard motorcycle test or when upgrading to a bigger bike.

Finally, the police take an active role in encouraging advanced rider training. BikeSafe workshops are well established, and run by many forces all over the UK. A typical workshop includes sessions on hazard awareness and safer riding, followed by a one-to-one assessment ride.

Glossary

Annual Percentage Rate (APR) – Interest rate on financial loans, the amount you will pay per year. Enables you to compare the cost of different loans.

Comprehensive insurance – Insurance policy which covers damage to your own bike in the event of an accident.

Compulsory Basic Training (CBT) – Basic riding skills qualification, which must be passed before taking the motorcycle Theory and Practical tests.

Driving Standards Agency (DSA) – Department for Transport section responsible for rider/driver training and tests.

European Health Insurance Card (EHIC) – Entitles the holder to medical treatment throughout the EU.

Fairing – Front bodywork, protecting bike and rider from the weather.

Front forks – Front suspension system.

Full-face helmet – Helmet with chin protection.

Get On – www.geton.co.uk. Website for new riders run by the Motorcycle Industry Association, with lots of useful information, including free test rides.

Goretex – Waterproof/breathable lining, used in jackets, trousers, gloves and boots.

Guaranteed Future Value (GFV) – See PCP below. GFV is the bike's agreed value at the end of the PCP term.

MoT – Annual safety check, compulsory for all bikes over three years old.

Personal Contract Package (PCP) – Financing scheme for new and recent used bikes. Lease the bike over a fixed period (usually three years) with an option to purchase at the end.

Practical test – Official riding test, with on-road and on-site.

Swingarm – Part of the rear suspension system, and the rear wheel mounting.

Tax disc – Officially, the Road Fund Licence, which pays for your use of the roads. This must be displayed on the bike.

Theory test – Screen-based multiple choice and hazard perception tests. This must be passed before you can take the Practical test.

Third Party, Fire & Theft Insurance – Insurance policy covering third party claims, and your bike against theft and fire damage.

Third Party Only Insurance – Insurance policy covering third party claims only. The legal minimum cover.

Twist-and-go – Fully automatic transmission as on a scooter.

Two-up – Riding with a pillion passenger.

V5C – Registration document, with details of the bike and the registered keeper. You must have this to use the bike on the road.

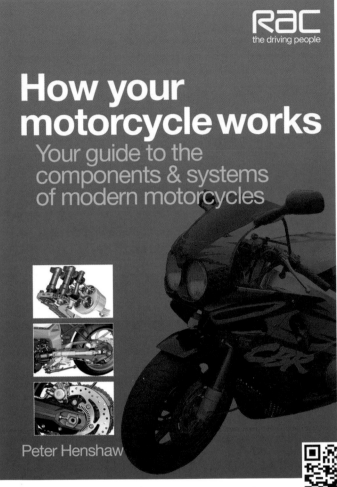

Index